MACHINES RULE!

IN THE AIR

Steve Parker

Smart Apple Media

Smart Apple Media
P.O. Box 3263
Mankato, Minnesota 56002

Printed in the United States.

Published by arrangement with the Watts Publishing Group Ltd, London.

Library of Congress Cataloging-in-Publication Data

Parker, Steve, 1976-
  In the air / Steve Parker.
      p. cm.—(Machines rule!)
  Includes bibliographical references and index.
  Summary: "Covers a wide selection of machines that fly, from airliners
  to hot air balloons, outlining how they work and their uses"–Provided
  by publisher.
  ISBN 978-1-59920-284-6 (hardcover)
  1. Aeronautics—Juvenile literature. 2. Airplanes—Juvenile literature.
  I. Title.
  TL547.P2725 2010
  629.13–dc22

                                                    200804449

Editor: Jeremy Smith
Design: Billin Design Solutions
Art director: Jonathan Hair

Picture credits: Agencia Mendoza/Sygma/Corbis: 21br. © Airbus SAS. All
rights reserved: 8bl, 8br, 9tr, 9bl, 9br, 16b. Stephan
Aufschnalter/epa/Corbis: 12b.Bettmann/Corbis: 26t. © Boeing Company. All
rights reserved: 7t, 10t, 10b, 14b, 15bl, 15tr, 18, 19bl, 19br, 22-23c, 28-
29, 30. Gary James Calder/Shutterstock: 13tr. Lance Cheung/USAF/Topfoto:
11br. Dan/Shutterstock : 21tl. Dryden Flight Research Center/NASA: 27tl.
Joerge Ferrari/epa/Corbis: 4-5, 13b. S. Feval/Le Matin/Sygmas/Corbis:
21bl. James Fraser/Rex Features: 11tr. Timothy E. Goodwin/Shutterstock:
7c. H. Goussé © Airbus SAS. All rights reserved: 8-9. George Hall/Corbis:
16t. Stephen Hind/Reuters/Corbis: 1. Robert Kyllo/Shutterstock : 17b.
Langley Research Center/NASA: 27b, 27tr, 27br. David Le
Bon/Transtock/Corbis : 17c. © Lockheed Martin Corporation. All rights
reserved: front cover t, 2, 3, 6, 14t, 15tl, 15br, 19t, 20, 23t, 23b, 25tl, 26b.
Peter MacDiarmid/Rex Features: 25bl. Elizabeth Opalenik/Corbis: 21tr, 31.
Rex Features: 11tl. Dibyangshu Sarkar/AFP/Getty Images: 24, 25tr.
Skyscan/Corbis: 12t, 13tl. Jim Sugar/Corbis : front cover br, 7b. Todd
Taulman/Shutterstock : front cover bl. UNSCOM/Corbis: 22b. US Navy ©
Boeing Company. All rights reserved: 25br. US Navy/Ensign John Gray ©
Boeing Company. All rights reserved: 11bl. Robin Utrecht/ANP/epa/Corbis:
17t.   Brad Whitsitt/Shutterstock: 17tr.

Words in **bold** or ***bold italics*** can be found in the glossary on page 28.

CONTENTS

Blast Off!

The engines roar, the power surges, the wheels rumble, and the wings tremble. Up, up, and away you go into the clear sky. Get ready for takeoff on an exciting journey through the air.

There are many different types of aircraft. Jet planes take people on vacation all over the world. Helicopters can hover in the air and are used by armies and emergency services. Spy planes and fighter planes protect countries while stunt planes allow pilots to show off their skills!

Military Planes

Most countries have an **air force**. Fighter planes can help defeat enemy aircraft while "invisible" spy planes can spot other aircraft without being seen themselves.

Helicopters

Helicopters can be used to perform many tasks. They can haul people, cargo, or mass weapons. They are also used by air forces all over the world.

Airplanes

Many people travel by airplane. These planes range from small airplanes to commercial jets that can carry hundreds of people at a time.

Stunt Planes

If pilots want to show off their skills for fun, they fly stunt planes. These planes can go upside down and spin around and much more!

Airliners

The biggest planes in the world are airliners. The original airliner was the Boeing 747, which first flew more than 30 years ago. The newest airliner is the Airbus A380.

The A380 is a double-decker, with two floors all along the **fuselage**. One version can carry 800 people in standard class. The other seats 520 in first, business, and standard classes.

The brand new A380 airbus was launched to a fanfare of music, flashing lights, and fountains of water from special airport fire engines.

Stats and Facts

THAT'S INCREDIBLE
The A380 is unlikely to damage runways because it has 22 wheels, four more than a Boeing 747.

Airbus A380

Maker: Airbud (European)

Length: 239.5 ft (73 m)

Wing Span: 261.8 ft (79.8 m)

Height: 79 ft (24.1 m)

Empty Weight: 275 tons (250 t)

Full Weight: 650 tons (590 t)

Engines: 4 Rolls Royce Trent 970/977's or EA GP7, 200's

Cruising Speed: 559 mph (900 km/h)

Test pilots first flew the A380 in April 2005.

The jet engine has a massive fan with blades on it.

There is plenty of room to relax in a first class seat!

Attack Aircraft

Missiles

Attack aircraft are the cutting edge of today's air forces. They fly deep into enemy land and stay low to avoid *radar*. Then they deliver their radar-guided or heat-seeking missiles and laser-guided bombs, and roar back to safety.

The F-15 Eagle is one of the world's best all-weather attack aircraft. The attack pilot sits in front. The rear seat is for the Weapons Systems Officer (WSO), nicknamed "wizzo".

THAT'S INCREDIBLE
The F-15E Eagle can blast straight upwards at the rate of 273 yds (250 m) every second!

Stats and Facts

F-15E Strike Eagle

Maker: McDonnell Douglas/ Boeing (USA)

Length: 63.7 ft (19.4 m)

Wing Span: 42.7 ft (13 m)

Height: 8.3 ft (5.6 m)

Empty Weight: 15.4 tons (14 t)

Full Weight: 39 tons (36 t)

Engines: 2 Pratt & Whitney F100-299's

Top Speed: 1,671 mph (2,690 km/h)

Missiles and bombs (above) are stored under the wings.

As the jet engines boost the attack aircraft through the **sound barrier**, shock waves form and make a sonic boom that sounds like thunder.

Fighter pilots wear helmets with oxygen masks to help them breathe.

Stunt Planes

The highlight of any air show is a display by a stunt plane. Loops, rolls, and dives thrill the crowd. Then the colored smoke switches on and the plane makes amazing patterns in the sky.

The Extra 300 is a hugely successful aerobatic **monoplane** (it has one set of wings). The wings give the same lifting force whether the plane is right way up or upside down.

Flying in close formation takes great skill.

Stats and Facts

THAT'S INCREDIBLE

A stunt plane can twirl or spin around in less than a second.

Extra 300

Maker: Extra Flugzeugbau (Germany)

Length: 22.6 ft (6.9 m)

Wing Span: 24.3 ft (7.4 m)

Height: 8.5 ft (2.6 m)

Empty Weight: 1,500 lbs (680 kg)

Full Weight: 2,090 lbs (950 kg)

Engine: AEIO-540 L1B5

Extra 300 pilots get used to performing incredible stunts. They can spin around and turn upside down, although pilots may be sick at first!

Planes race around a circuit marked out by tall blow-up pylons.

Stealth Planes

How can a plane be invisible? *Stealth planes* are, but only on a radar screen. Radar is used to detect aircraft. Stealth technology makes planes invisible to the enemy's radar.

The F-22 Raptor stealth fighter joined the U.S. Air Force in 2005. The angle of the gas blast from its jet engines can be altered for faster twists and turns, which is called thrust vectoring.

The B-2 Spirit stealth bomber is one of the strangest shapes in the sky.

Radar uses radio waves that bounce back off an aircraft. But the B-2's shape means the radio waves bounce away at all angles and can't be detected.

THAT'S INCREDIBLE
The B-2 Spirit stealth bomber is the world's most costly airplane. You'd need more than $2 billion to buy one—if it were allowed.

The F–II7 Nighthawk fighter was one of the first stealth planes.

Stats and Facts

B-2 Spirit stealth bomber

Maker: Northrop Grumman (USA)

Length: 68.6 ft (20.9 m)

Wing Span: 170.9 ft (52.1 m)

Height: 16.7 ft (5.1 m)

Empty Weight: 77 tons (70 t)

Full Weight: 165 tons (150 t)

Engines: 4 General Electric F118-GE-100's

Top Speed: 472 mph (760 km/h)

In the air traffic control room, each "blip" on the screen is an aircraft. But stealth planes produce no blips at all.

Private Jets

If you want to go somewhere faraway and fast, take the plane! But if you want luxury, you need your own private plane like a Learjet (below), complete with pilot and copilot, and a crew to attend to your every need.

THAT'S INCREDIBLE

To hire a private jet usually costs at least $2,000 per hour. That's cheaper than buying one, however. They cost around $10 million!

Inside, the private jet is like a luxury suite.

Stats and Facts

"Welcome aboard!" If it is safe, you can have a chat with the pilot and look at the dials and controls.

Learjet 45XR

Maker: Bombadier (USA)

Length: 58.4 ft (17.8 m)

Wing Span: 47.9 ft (14.6 m)

Height: 14 ft (4.3 m)

Empty Weight: 6.8 tons (6.2 t)

Full Weight: 10 tons (9.5 t)

Engines: 2 Honeywell TFE71's

Cruising Speed: 521 mph (840 km/h)

A Learjet's tanks hold 70 times more fuel than a family car.

Private jets aren't always small. This Boeing 747, called Air Force One, is a private jet used by the president of the United States.

Attack Helicopters

Guns
Missiles

Rockets

The AH-64 Apache is one of the world's most fearsome fighting machines. This attack helicopter is loaded with guns, rockets, and missiles, and it can fly and land almost anywhere.

Stats and Facts

The Apache carries its weapons on the side of the helicopter.

AH-64 Apache

Maker: Hughes/Boeing/ McDonnell Douglas (USA)

Length: 58 ft (17.7 m)

Rotorspan: 47.9 ft (14.6 m)

Height: 12.4 ft (3.8 m)

Empty Weight: 5.6 tons (5.1 t)

Full Weight: 10.4 tons (9.5 t)

Engines: 2 General Electric T700-GE-701's

Cruising Speed: 167 mph (270 km/h)

THAT'S INCREDIBLE

The Apache Longbow can fire its missiles accurately even while it is hiding out of sight behind a hill!

The pilot's screens shows all kinds of infomation, from height and speed to how much fuel is left.

Apaches hover low over an airfield, ready to fire their rockets. Luckily this is just a practice to test the equipment.

Airships and Balloons

How do airships and balloons fly if they don't have wings? Airships are powered by a gas called *helium*, and they have engines and propellers. Balloons are usually round and have no engines. They fly using just hot air.

The big part of an airship is filled with helium.
The passengers sit in the cabin, or gondola, underneath.

Gondola

Stats and Facts

The Skyship 600 is a 14-seat airship powered by twin Porsche engines. It can travel up to 40 mph (65 km/h), at a height of around 437 yds (400 m). This airship can fly for an amazing 15 hours a day without refuelling.

Skyship 600

Maker: Global Skyship Industries (USA)

Length: 216.5 ft (66 m)

Volume: 268,391 ft^3 (7,600 m^3)

Height: 72.2 ft (22 m)

Weight: 6 tons (5.5 t)

Personnel: Pilot, co-pilot, 12 passengers

Engines: 2 Turbo charged Porsche 930's or Textron Lycoming 10-540's

Cruising Speed: 40 mph (65 km/h)

A balloon contains hot air, which is lighter than cold air and floats upwards.

THAT'S INCREDIBLE

Steve Fossett made more long-distance balloon trips than anyone else. In 2002, he flew solo nonstop around the world by balloon.

Airlifters

Cargo, freight, and transport aircraft are known as airlifters. They must be strong, tough, and easy to take off and land, because their runways are not always very smooth.

nose

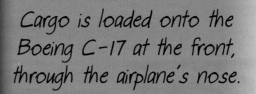

Cargo is loaded onto the Boeing C-17 at the front, through the airplane's nose.

Stats and Facts

The C-5 Galaxy can carry the same weight as 1,700 people, or three battle tanks.

THAT'S INCREDIBLE

The Galaxy's cargo compartment is so big that the entire Wright Brothers' airplane from 1903 could fit into it!

C-5 Galaxy

Maker: Lockheed (USA)

Length: 247.4 ft (75.3 m)

Wing Span: 222.8 ft (67.9 m)

Height: 65 ft (19.8 m)

Empty Weight: 187 tons (170 t)

Full Weight: 418 tons (380 t)

Engines: 4 General Electric TF39's

Cruising Speed: 559 mph (900 km/h)

The C-130 Hercules is the most successful airlifter. It is used by air forces and airlines as a cargo carrier in more than 50 countries.

Jump Jets

Jump jets are fighter planes that can take off by going straight up and land by coming straight down. This is called VTOL—Vertical Takeoff and Landing.

Nozzles

The Harrier is the most famous jump jet. Air for the Harrier jump jet's engine enters the filters on the side of the plane. Four moveable **nozzles** direct the jet blast downward for takeoff and landing, and backward for level flight.

THAT'S INCREDIBLE

The Harrier has starred in more films than any other plane, from the James Bond film *Living Daylights* to *True Lies*, starring Arnold Schwarzenegger.

Stats and Facts

Harrier II

Maker: British Aerospace (UK)
Boeing/McDonnell Douglas (USA)

Length: 46.3 ft (14.1 m)

Wing Span: 30.2 ft (9.2 m)

Height: 11.5 ft (3.5 m)

Empty Weight: 6.3 tons (5.7 t)

Full Weight: 9.4 tons (8.5 t)

Engines: Rolls Royce Pegasus 105

Cruising Speed: 621 mph
(1,000 km/h)

Harriers take off and land anywhere, from a woodland clearing to the swaying deck of an aircraft carrier.

The F-35 Lighting II lands vertically using a large, down-facing fan-propeller.

The V-22 Osprey has engines and propellers at its wing ends. These face up for vertical takeoff, then swing around to point forward for normal flight.

Record Breakers

Fastest, highest, longest—the world of aircraft
is full of amazing records and feats.
Here are some from over the years.

The Concorde was
the world's only
passenger plane
that could fly faster than
sound. It could cruise at
1,305 mph (2,100 km/h). It first
flew in 1969 and retired in 2003.

The SR-71A Blackbird spy plane
flew faster and higher than any
other civilian or military aircraft.
In 1976, it set the world speed
record of 2,193 mph (3,529 km/h)
and the height record of
85,069 ft (25,929 m).

THAT'S INCREDIBLE

The longest wings on any aircraft are on the Hughes H-4 "Spruce Goose," a one-off giant seaplane with a 320 ft (97.54 m) wingspan!

Stats and Facts

The X-15 was the United States' last experimental "X plane." It was not so much an aircraft as it was a rocket with wings and a pilot. It flew faster than 4,474 mph (7,200 km/h) in 1967.

X-15

Maker: North American Aviation (USA)

Length: 50.9 ft (15.5 m)

Wing Span: 22.3 ft (6.8 m)

Height: 13.5 ft (4.1 m)

Empty Weight: 7.3 tons (6,620 kg)

Full Weight: 17 tons (15,420 kg)

Engines: XLR-99 Rocket Engine

Max Speed: 4,519 mph (7,274 km/h)

The fastest propeller plane was the Grumman F8F Bearcat, at 528 mph (850 km/h).

The Bell X-1 rocket plane was the first aircraft to go supersonic (faster than sound) in 1947.

Glossary

Air force
Part of a country's military that can attack or defend from the air.

Airlifter
A very large aircraft that can carry extremely heavy loads.

Fan
The spinning, many-bladed part at the front of a plane, which takes in air for the engine and works as a propeller in a jet engine.

Formation
When aircraft fly near each other, forming an overall pattern such as a V or X.

Fuselage
The main body of an aircraft, which is usually long and tube-shaped.

Helium
A lighter-than-air gas, used in airships and some balloons (also found in some party balloons).

Loop
When a plane goes up and over on its back, upside down, and then comes down to fly level again, tracing a circle in the sky.

Monoplane
An aircraft with one pair of main wings, left and right, rather than a double pair as in a biplane.

Nozzle
A hole or tapering tube on a jet engine that alters the direction of the jet blast.

Radar
Sending out radio waves to bounce off objects, then detecting the returning echoes to find the direction, distance and size of the object. Radar stands for Radio Detection And Ranging.

Roll
When a plane tilts one wing down and the other up and keeps going, twisting around in the sky.

Stealth plane
An aircraft which is difficult to detect in various ways—on a radar screen, from its noise, from the radio signals it sends out, and from the heat in its engines.

Sound barrier
When an aircraft flies faster than the speed of sound, it "breaks the sound barrier" and causes a deep thud or sonic boom.

Test pilot
A very skillful pilot who flies the first versions of an aircraft to check that it all works well, is safe, and flies properly.

VTOL
Vertical Take Off and Landing. A plane that can take off by going straight up and land by coming straight down.

Web Sites

http://www.howstuffworks.com/airplane.htm
Explanations about how all kinds of aircraft and their parts work.

http://www.century-of-flight.net/
Huge site celebrating 100 years of aircraft, mainly for older children.

http://inventors.about.com/library/inventors/blhowajetengineworks.htm
How different kinds of jet engines work.

http://www.heliphotos.co.uk/works.htm
How helicopters fly and are controlled.

http://www.planepictures.net/
Plenty of pictures of all kinds of planes.

Further Reading

Aircraft (How Machines Work) by Ian Graham, Smart Apple Media, 2009

Planes in Action (On the Go) by David and Penny Glover, PowerKids Press, 2008

Planes (Extreme Machines) by David Jefferis, Smart Apple Media, 2008

Planes (Transportation Around the World) by Chris Oxlade, Heinemann Library, 2008

Note to Parents and Teachers:

Every effort has been made by the publishers to ensure that the web sites in this book are suitable for children, that they are of the highest educational value, and that they contain no inappropriate or offensive material. However, because of the nature of the Internet, it is impossible to guarantee that the contents of these sites will not be altered. We strongly advise that Internet access is supervised by a responsible adult.

Index

A

aerobatic planes 12–13
AH-64 Apache 18–19
Airbus A380 8–9
Air Force One 17
airlifters 22-23
airships 20–21
Attack Aircraft 10–11

B

B-2 Spirit stealth bomber 14, 15
balloons 20–21
Bell-X1 rocket plane 27
Boeing 747 8, 9, 17
Boeing C-17 22

C

C-5 Galaxy 23
C-130 Hercules 23
Concorde 26

E

Extra 300 12–13

F

F8F Bearcat 27
F-15E Eagle 11
F-22 Raptor stealth fighter 14
F-35 Lighting II 25
F-117 Nighthawk fighter 15

H

Harrier jump jet 24–25
helicopters 6, 7, 18–19
Hughes H-4 27

L

Learjet 45XR 17

M

monoplane 12

P

private jets 16–17

R

radar 10, 14, 15, 19

S

Skyship 600 21
sound barrier 11, 27
spy planes 14–15, 26
SR-71A Blackbird 6, 26
stealth planes 14–15
stunt planes 7, 12–13
supersonic 27

V

Vertical Take Off and Landing (VTOL) 24–25
V-22 Osprey 25

X

X-15 27